# The Battle for America

Inside the 2024 Election

Daniel George

Table of Contents

# Introduction

## The Significance of 2024

As the 2024 U.S. election draws near, the nation faces a pivotal moment that could redefine its future. This election goes beyond merely selecting a president; it encapsulates the core values and direction of the country amid growing challenges and societal divisions.

In a time when misinformation is rampant and media narratives heavily influence public opinion, grasping the nuances of this election is crucial. Candidates are not just presenting their visions; they are engaged in a fierce contest for the allegiance of a diverse and often divided electorate.

This book seeks to unravel the complexities surrounding the 2024 election, providing insights into the leading candidates, their tactics, and the key events that will shape the campaign. From the high-stakes debates that capture public attention to the vital swing states that could decide the election, we will examine the factors that affect voter choices.

Moreover, we will explore the media's role as both a platform for candidates and a battleground for shaping perceptions. The outcome of the 2024 election will be determined not only by votes cast but also by the narratives created in news cycles and social media platforms.

As we explore the dynamics of this election, we invite you to join us in understanding the intricate factors at play. Together, we will uncover the stories that will influence America's future, aiming to provide a holistic view of what this election signifies for the nation.

Prepare to delve into the complexities of the 2024 election, analyzing the critical issues, debates, and moments that will shape the outcome and the future of American democracy. This journey is not merely a recounting of events; it is an exploration of the ideas, passions, and challenges that define our current political climate.

# Chapter 1

## Key Players and Their Platforms

As the 2024 U.S. presidential election approaches, the contest is set between two prominent candidates: Vice President Kamala Harris and former President Donald Trump. This chapter delves into their backgrounds, political philosophies, and the platforms they advocate to garner voter support.

## Kamala Harris: Advocate for Progressive Reform

Kamala Harris, representing the Democratic Party, has built her campaign around progressive values that resonate with many Americans seeking meaningful change. As the first woman of color to hold the vice presidency, she emphasizes inclusivity and social justice. Key issues in her platform include:

- Universal Healthcare: Harris champions expanding access to affordable healthcare through a public option, advocating for the belief that healthcare should be a fundamental right. She aims to address disparities that exist in healthcare access across different demographics.

- Environmental Policy: Harris prioritizes combating climate change, proposing initiatives that include transitioning to renewable energy sources and investing in sustainable job creation. She calls for significant legislation to tackle environmental challenges head-on.

- Criminal Justice Reform: With a background as a prosecutor, Harris emphasizes reforming the criminal justice system to address systemic racism and mass incarceration. She advocates for community-focused policing and policies that uplift marginalized groups.

Mobilizing younger voters, especially those passionate about progressive causes, is essential for Harris's success. Her challenge lies in unifying the Democratic base, which consists of both moderates and progressives with differing views.

## Donald Trump: The Populist Challenger

On the other side, Donald Trump stands as the Republican nominee, known for his populist approach that resonates with voters feeling disenfranchised by conventional politics. His platform is characterized by:

- Economic Nationalism: Trump focuses on protecting American jobs and industries through "America First" trade policies. He advocates for tariffs on imports and reducing regulations to promote economic growth, appealing to working-class citizens.

- Strict Immigration Policies: Immigration control is a cornerstone of Trump's platform. He promotes border security measures, including the construction of a wall, and seeks to reduce illegal immigration through stringent enforcement.

- Cultural Conservatism: Trump presents himself as a defender of traditional American values, often criticizing what he sees as a decline in societal norms. He appeals to evangelical voters and those concerned about gun rights, religious liberties, and liberal overreach.

Trump's campaign strategy is grounded in energizing his loyal base, yet he faces the challenge of broadening his appeal to moderate Republicans and independents who may be skeptical of his divisive rhetoric.

## The Ideological Divide

The stark contrast between Harris and Trump highlights a broader ideological conflict within the country. Harris advocates for progressive reforms addressing systemic issues, while Trump promotes a populist agenda focused on economic growth and traditional values.

This election will serve as a critical referendum on these divergent visions, reflecting the priorities of the American electorate. Topics like healthcare, climate change, economic recovery, and social justice will dominate discussions and shape voter perceptions of each candidate.

As we navigate the upcoming election cycle, understanding how these candidates articulate their platforms and tackle pressing national challenges is crucial. The choices made by voters will not only determine the election's outcome but will also influence the future direction of American policies and society.

In subsequent chapters, we will explore the campaign strategies employed by both candidates, the swing states crucial to the election, and significant events that will shape this historic race. Grasping the motivations, obstacles, and aspirations of these candidates is essential as we brace for an unforgettable election season.

# Chapter 2

## The Political Landscape and Key Issues

As the 2024 presidential election approaches, the political landscape in the United States is shaped by several crucial issues that will significantly influence voter behavior. Candidates must navigate this intricate environment, responding to the concerns that resonate most with the electorate.

## Economic Recovery and Stability

The economy remains a primary concern for voters, especially in light of the COVID-19 pandemic's lingering effects. Issues such as inflation, job security, and economic inequality are at the forefront of public discourse. Candidates are expected to present clear, actionable strategies to restore economic growth and stability.

- Inflation Concerns: The rising cost of living, particularly in essential goods and services, has led to widespread concern among voters. Candidates must articulate how they intend to manage inflation and stabilize prices. This could involve implementing fiscal policies that control spending, enhancing supply chain efficiency, and supporting measures that protect consumer purchasing power.

- Job Creation and Workforce Development: The pandemic resulted in significant job losses, making the creation of new employment opportunities crucial. Candidates need to outline their plans for job creation, focusing on infrastructure investments, support for small businesses, and initiatives that target emerging industries. Additionally, addressing workforce development is essential, as many individuals require reskilling to adapt to the evolving job market.

## Social Justice and Equity

The national dialogue surrounding social justice has evolved, with increasing public awareness of systemic inequalities. Key issues include racial justice, gender equity, and LGBTQ+ rights, and voters expect candidates to take definitive stances on these topics.

- Racial Equity Initiatives: The demand for racial justice has gained momentum, especially following high-profile incidents of police violence and systemic discrimination. Candidates must demonstrate their commitment to addressing these issues through policies that promote equity in education, healthcare, and economic opportunities.

- Criminal Justice Reform: Many voters are concerned about the impact of the criminal justice system on marginalized communities. Candidates advocating for reforms—such as reducing mass incarceration, promoting restorative justice practices, and improving community policing—will likely resonate with those seeking meaningful change.

## Healthcare Access

Healthcare remains a top priority for many Americans, particularly in light of the pandemic's emphasis on the need for a strong healthcare system. Candidates must address the imperative of providing accessible and affordable healthcare.

- Increasing Accessibility: As healthcare costs rise, voters seek candidates who can offer solutions that enhance access to quality medical services. This could involve supporting Medicaid expansion, increasing subsidies for health insurance, and instituting price controls on prescription medications.

- Mental Health Services: The pandemic has exacerbated mental health challenges for many individuals, heightening the demand for mental health services. Candidates must acknowledge the significance of comprehensive mental health care and propose initiatives that integrate these services into the broader healthcare system.

## Climate Change and Environmental Policy

With the impact of climate change becoming more apparent, voters are increasingly concerned about environmental issues. Candidates are expected to address climate change and propose viable strategies for sustainability.

- Promoting Renewable Energy: Transitioning to renewable energy sources is critical for addressing climate change. Candidates who advocate for clean energy initiatives—such as investments in solar and wind energy and enhancements in energy efficiency—are likely to attract environmentally conscious voters.

- Environmental Justice: The connection between environmental issues and social justice is gaining prominence among the electorate. Candidates who recognize the disproportionate effects of environmental degradation on marginalized communities and propose equitable solutions will be viewed favorably.

## The Challenge of Misinformation

In the digital age, misinformation poses a significant obstacle to informed electoral choices. Candidates must navigate this complex landscape and ensure that their messages resonate above the noise.

- Strategies Against Misinformation: With social media playing a pivotal role in shaping public opinion, candidates need to develop effective strategies to counter misinformation. This includes promoting transparency, providing accurate information, and engaging directly with communities to build trust.

## Conclusion

The 2024 election represents a critical juncture for the United States, reflecting the priorities and concerns of its citizens. Candidates must engage with key issues such as economic recovery, social justice, healthcare access, climate change, and misinformation to effectively connect with voters. Understanding this political landscape is essential as candidates navigate their campaigns and seek to resonate with a diverse electorate.

As we progress through this election cycle, it will be important to closely monitor how these issues develop and how candidates respond. The choices made by voters will not only determine the election's outcome but also shape the nation's future direction. With high stakes involved, the engagement of the electorate is more critical than ever.

# Chapter 3

## The Significance of Key Issues in the 2024 Election

As we approach the 2024 presidential election, various critical issues are shaping voter sentiments and influencing candidate strategies. The positions taken by candidates on these topics will not only define their campaigns but also affect how they are perceived by the electorate.

## Economic Recovery and Employment

The economic situation is a primary concern for many voters, especially in the aftermath of the disruptions caused by the COVID-19 pandemic. Numerous Americans continue to deal with the repercussions, including unemployment, inflation, and increased living costs. Candidates must provide clear solutions to these pressing issues.

## Controlling Inflation

In recent years, inflation has escalated, resulting in higher prices for everyday items. Voters are particularly anxious about how these rising costs affect their lives, from grocery shopping to housing expenses. Candidates who can propose effective measures to curb inflation—through fiscal policies, improved supply chain management, and protecting consumer purchasing power—will connect with concerned citizens.

## Creating Job Opportunities

With the nation striving for economic recovery, the generation of new jobs is essential. Candidates need to outline realistic plans for job creation across various sectors, which might include significant infrastructure investments, small business support, and promoting innovation in technology and sustainable energy.

Additionally, addressing workforce development through reskilling initiatives is vital for equipping individuals for the evolving job market.

## Social Justice and Inclusion

Social justice issues have gained increasing prominence, with many voters emphasizing the need for equity and inclusion. Candidates must thoughtfully engage with these topics to foster trust and connection with constituents.

## Commitment to Racial Justice

The pursuit of racial equity has intensified, particularly in response to high-profile events that exposed systemic racism. Candidates are expected to present policies that tackle racial disparities in education, healthcare, and economic opportunity. Effective advocacy for racial justice will resonate with voters seeking substantial reforms.

## Reforming the Criminal Justice System

The push for reforms in the criminal justice system continues to grow, driven by a heightened awareness of its effects on marginalized groups. Candidates prioritizing initiatives such as reducing mass incarceration, implementing restorative justice practices, and improving community policing will likely gain support from those advocating for social justice.

## Access to Healthcare

Healthcare remains a pivotal issue for the electorate, especially as the pandemic has underscored the need for a strong healthcare system. Voters increasingly demand candidates address the challenges of providing accessible and affordable healthcare.

## Improving Healthcare Accessibility

With many Americans struggling to afford healthcare, candidates must propose solutions to enhance access to quality medical services. This could include advocating for Medicaid expansion, increasing subsidies for health insurance, and instituting price controls on prescription medications.

## Emphasizing Mental Health Services

The pandemic has heightened awareness of the need for mental health resources, as individuals face unprecedented challenges. Candidates should prioritize mental health care by proposing initiatives that integrate these services into the healthcare system, ensuring accessibility for all.

## Climate Change and Environmental Stewardship

The urgency of addressing climate change has emerged as a defining issue in politics today. As environmental concerns take center stage, candidates must present credible sustainability plans.

## Advocating for Renewable Energy

Making the switch to renewable energy sources is crucial to reducing global warming. Candidates who support clean energy initiatives—such as investments in solar and wind power—will likely attract environmentally conscious voters. Proposing policies that enhance energy efficiency and reduce carbon emissions will also be crucial in appealing to this demographic.

## Focusing on Environmental Justice

Recognizing the link between environmental and social justice is increasingly vital. Candidates who address the disproportionate impact of environmental issues on marginalized communities will gain credibility with voters seeking equitable solutions. Advocating for policies that safeguard vulnerable populations from environmental hazards can enhance a candidate's appeal.

## Combating Misinformation

In the digital era, misinformation presents a significant obstacle to informed electoral choices. Candidates must navigate this complex terrain and ensure their messages resonate amidst the noise.

## Strategies to Address Misinformation

As social media influences public perception, candidates need to develop effective tactics to counter misinformation. This includes promoting transparency, disseminating factual information, and directly engaging with communities to build trust. By confronting misinformation, candidates can help cultivate a more informed electorate.

## Conclusion

The key issues shaping the 2024 election are intricately linked to the concerns of American voters. As candidates engage with topics such as economic recovery, social justice, healthcare access, climate change, and misinformation, their ability to connect with the electorate will be vital. Understanding these issues is crucial for candidates and voters alike as they navigate the complexities of this pivotal election, which will have lasting implications for the nation's trajectory.

# Chapter 4

## The Significance of Voter Engagement and Mobilization in the 2024 Election

As the 2024 election nears, grasping the dynamics of voter engagement and mobilization is essential. The effectiveness of candidates hinges not only on their policies but also on their capacity to energize supporters and encourage active participation in the electoral process. This chapter delves into the strategies and trends influencing voter engagement, the impact of grassroots movements, and the importance of tackling voter disenfranchisement.

## Understanding Voter Engagement

Voter engagement encompasses the methods and tactics designed to stimulate individuals' participation in elections, from registration to actual voting. Factors like social media, community outreach, and the overall political environment significantly influence voter engagement.

## The Role of Social Media

Social media has transformed how candidates connect with potential voters, providing a platform for direct communication. This allows candidates to share their messages, rally support, and initiate grassroots campaigns. Engaging content, such as videos and infographics, resonates particularly well with younger voters who often rely on digital channels for information.

## Community Outreach Initiatives

Efforts to engage communities through door-to-door canvassing, phone banking, and town hall meetings remain vital for motivating voters. Candidates who prioritize building relationships in their communities tend to foster trust and inspire increased participation. Grassroots organizations often play a crucial role by organizing events that unite voters and create a sense of belonging.

## The Influence of Grassroots Movements

Grassroots movements wield significant influence over electoral outcomes, especially at local and state levels. These movements typically arise from a collective concern within communities, advocating for changes on issues such as healthcare, climate action, and social justice.

## Mobilizing the Base

Grassroots organizations are essential in mobilizing supporters, encouraging them to register, vote, and advocate for meaningful issues. They often employ innovative strategies, including peer-to-peer texting and targeted social media outreach, to engage potential voters effectively. Mobilizing the base is especially crucial in energizing those who may feel disillusioned or disconnected from the political process.

## Building Coalitions

Forming coalitions among various grassroots organizations can amplify voices and enhance impact. By uniting different groups around shared objectives, coalitions can draw attention to important issues and gather broader support. For example, collaborations between environmental, labor, and social justice organizations can bolster advocacy for comprehensive climate policies while addressing economic inequality.

## Addressing Voter Disenfranchisement

Despite advancements in voter engagement, challenges persist regarding disenfranchisement, particularly among marginalized communities. Efforts to suppress voter turnout—through strict voter ID laws, purging of voter rolls, and gerrymandering—continue to hinder access to the electoral process.

## Strategies for Combatting Disenfranchisement

Candidates and advocacy groups must actively combat voter disenfranchisement by promoting accessible voting practices. This includes advocating for measures like automatic voter registration, early voting, and mail-in ballots. Raising awareness about these options can empower individuals who may otherwise face barriers to exercising their voting rights.

## Educating Voters

Education is vital in addressing disenfranchisement. Providing clear information about voter rights, the voting process, and the significance of participation can inspire confidence and motivate engagement. Voter education initiatives can be particularly effective in communities historically facing obstacles to participation.

## The Importance of Turnout

Voter turnout ultimately determines whether an election is successful. Higher participation rates indicate a healthy democracy and reflect the electorate's engagement in the political process. Candidates who can effectively mobilize supporters, address disenfranchisement, and inspire individuals to vote will hold a significant advantage in the 2024 election.

## Conclusion

As the 2024 election approaches, the significance of voter engagement and mobilization cannot be overstated. Candidates must navigate the complexities of a changing political landscape while addressing the needs of the electorate. By employing innovative strategies, prioritizing grassroots movements, and working to eliminate voter disenfranchisement, they can foster a more engaged and empowered voter base, ultimately shaping the election's outcome and the nation's future.

# Chapter 5

## The Importance of Political Issues in the 2024 Election

As the 2024 election approaches, several pressing issues are shaping the political landscape and influencing voter sentiment. This chapter explores critical topics, including healthcare, the economy, climate change, and social justice, highlighting how candidates position themselves and the impact these issues have on voter behavior.

## Major Political Issues

Numerous significant issues have emerged as focal points in the 2024 election cycle, impacting both candidate platforms and voter priorities.

## Healthcare

Healthcare continues to be a major concern for many Americans, with ongoing discussions around access, affordability, and quality of care. Candidates are expected to address issues like rising prescription drug costs, the future of the Affordable Care Act, and potential healthcare reforms. The COVID-19 pandemic has emphasized the need for a robust healthcare system, leading voters to closely scrutinize candidates' proposals for enhancing public health.

## The Economy

The economy remains a central theme in elections, gaining increased attention due to inflation and economic uncertainty. Voters will focus on candidates' economic policies, including taxation, job creation, and support for small businesses. Those who present clear, actionable plans to tackle economic challenges will likely garner more support from constituents concerned about their financial stability.

## Climate Change

Climate change has swiftly risen on the political agenda, with voters demanding effective action to address environmental issues. Candidates will be assessed based on their commitment to sustainable practices, renewable energy initiatives, and comprehensive strategies for combating climate change. The influence of grassroots movements and youth activism has intensified calls for strong climate action, making this issue a crucial factor in voter mobilization.

## Social Justice and Equality

Social justice topics, including racial equality, gender rights, and LGBTQ+ advocacy, are pivotal in shaping voter priorities. Candidates' positions on these matters significantly influence their appeal to diverse voter demographics. The increasing awareness and activism surrounding these issues, fueled by movements such as Black Lives Matter and Me Too, have driven candidates to confront systemic inequalities and propose solutions for fostering inclusivity.

## Candidates' Reactions

Candidates must navigate these multifaceted issues while clearly articulating their positions. The ability to connect with voters on critical topics can greatly affect their success in both the primaries and the general election.

## Developing Compelling Messages

Effective candidates often tailor their messages to align with their constituents' concerns. This requires an understanding of the nuances surrounding each issue and presenting relatable narratives that connect with voters' experiences. Using personal stories and real-life examples can make candidates' messages more impactful and relatable.

## Engaging Voter Concerns

Candidates who engage with voters through town halls, social media, and community events build trust and foster connections. Directly addressing concerns and answering questions allows candidates to show their commitment to understanding and responding to the needs of their constituents.

## The Impact on Voter Behavior

Political issues significantly influence voter behavior, shaping preferences and determining turnout. Voters are more inclined to participate in elections when they feel strongly about the matters at stake.

## Mobilization through Issue Advocacy

Grassroots organizations and advocacy groups are crucial in mobilizing voters around specific issues. These groups raise awareness, educate constituents, and encourage participation in the electoral process. Their efforts can enhance voter turnout and engagement, particularly among younger and marginalized populations.

## The Power of Issue-Based Campaigns

Candidates focusing on issues that resonate with voters can create a compelling narrative that drives support. Issue-based campaigns foster urgency and importance, motivating individuals to vote and advocate for change.

## Conclusion

As the 2024 election approaches, political issues will significantly shape the electoral landscape. Candidates who effectively address voter concerns while presenting clear, actionable solutions will hold a considerable advantage. By understanding the key issues at play and engaging constituents actively, candidates can mobilize support and drive meaningful change. The intersection of political issues and voter engagement will be crucial in determining the nation's future.

# Chapter 6

## The Role of Media and Technology in the 2024 Election

As the 2024 election approaches, media and technology are vital in shaping political dialogue, influencing voter opinions, and rallying support for candidates. Understanding the evolving dynamics of media platforms and technological advancements is crucial for comprehending their impact on campaigns and voter engagement. This chapter delves into the significance of media, the rise of digital channels, the challenges posed by misinformation, and the role of data analytics in the electoral process.

## The Transformation of Political Media

Media has historically served as a powerful conduit for political communication, allowing candidates to share their messages and connect with voters. Traditional media platforms, such as television and radio, have been staples in political campaigns. However, the emergence of digital media has transformed candidate-voter interactions.

## The Impact of Traditional Media

Political campaigns are still dominated by television, which gives candidates a lot of publicity. Public views and beliefs are greatly influenced by political advertisements, news segments, and discussions on television. Radio is still helpful, especially when trying to reach listeners in far-flung locations.

## The Surge of Digital Media

Political communication has undergone a radical transformation thanks to digital media. Social media sites such as Facebook, Instagram, and Twitter allow candidates to interact with people in real time, provide updates, and mobilize support. This interpersonal bond fosters a sense of camaraderie among supporters and increases voter loyalty.

## The Challenge of Misinformation

While the digital landscape provides numerous advantages, it also brings challenges, particularly the proliferation of misinformation. False narratives and misleading claims can spread rapidly online, shaping voter opinions and potentially affecting electoral outcomes.

## Addressing Misinformation

Candidates and political entities must prioritize combating misinformation through transparency and fact-checking. Building credibility and trust is essential for navigating the pitfalls of misinformation and establishing rapport with voters.

## Data Analytics and Targeted Campaigning

These days, data analytics is crucial to modern political campaigns. Through the process of scrutinizing voter demographics, interests, and behaviors, candidates can successfully customize their approach and messaging.

## Understanding Voter Preferences

Campaigns can utilize data analytics to pinpoint key voter segments, allowing for more personalized engagement. Recognizing which issues resonate with specific demographics helps candidates craft messages that align with voter concerns, increasing the likelihood of mobilization.

## Targeted Advertising

Digital advertising allows campaigns to target particular audiences with tailored messages. By leveraging data, candidates can determine which platforms and messaging resonate most with specific groups, optimizing their outreach efforts for maximum engagement.

## The Power of Grassroots Digital Campaigning

Grassroots digital campaigning has emerged as a formidable force in mobilizing support and driving voter turnout. Engaging grassroots supporters through digital channels can amplify a candidate's message and foster a sense of ownership among constituents.

## Fostering Online Communities

Candidates can create online spaces where supporters share experiences, discuss issues, and mobilize action. These digital platforms allow grassroots supporters to connect with one another and the campaign, reinforcing community and commitment.

## Utilizing Peer-to-Peer Outreach

Peer-to-peer outreach via messaging platforms can enhance engagement and boost voter turnout. By encouraging supporters to reach out to their networks, candidates can leverage personal connections to motivate individuals to vote and advocate for the campaign.

## Conclusion

In the rapidly changing landscape of the 2024 election, the influence of media and technology is more significant than ever. Candidates must navigate the complexities of both traditional and digital media, address misinformation, and harness data analytics to engage voters effectively. By adopting innovative strategies and promoting grassroots digital campaigns, candidates can enhance their outreach efforts and rally support in ways that resonate with the electorate. The interplay between media, technology, and political engagement will ultimately shape the electoral landscape and impact the future of democracy in America.

# Chapter 7

## Mobilizing Voters through Grassroots Efforts

As the 2024 election draws closer, grassroots movements are increasingly crucial in fostering voter engagement and rallying support for candidates. This chapter explores the role of grassroots activism, effective strategies employed by these movements, and their influence on the electoral process.

## Defining Grassroots Movements

Grassroots movements are community-driven initiatives aimed at promoting change from the ground up. These efforts often arise in response to specific social, political, or economic challenges, reflecting local constituents' needs and concerns. The strength of grassroots activism lies in its capacity to unite individuals around shared goals, creating a strong sense of community.

## Key Features of Grassroots Movements

- Local Orientation: Grassroots movements generally focus on local issues, making them resonate with the unique needs of their communities.
- Diversity and Inclusion: These movements strive to include a wide range of voices, particularly those from marginalized communities, ensuring everyone has a chance to advocate for change.
- Community Engagement: Grassroots initiatives depend heavily on direct engagement with community members, utilizing local networks and events to galvanize support.

## Tactics for Successful Grassroots Engagement

Effective grassroots movements use various strategies to engage voters and encourage participation in the electoral process.

## Leveraging Social Media

Social media has become a vital tool for grassroots movements, facilitating rapid communication and organization. Candidates and activists can utilize these platforms to share information, rally supporters, and raise awareness about pressing issues.

- Developing Shareable Content: Creating engaging and easily shareable content is essential for reaching a broader audience. Memes, videos, and infographics can effectively convey messages and inspire action among supporters.
- Building Online Communities: Establishing online forums or groups allows supporters to connect, share their stories, and discuss relevant topics, fostering community and commitment.

## Hosting Events and Rallies

In-person gatherings, such as town halls, rallies, and community meetings, are vital for mobilizing grassroots support. These events provide opportunities for candidates and activists to connect directly with voters, address concerns, and cultivate relationships.

- Encouraging Attendance: Promoting events through social media, local media, and community organizations can enhance turnout and create urgency around critical issues.
- Engaging Local Influencers: Involving local leaders and influencers can amplify messaging and add credibility to grassroots initiatives.

## The Effect of Grassroots Movements on Voter Participation

Grassroots movements play a significant role in boosting voter turnout, especially among younger and marginalized populations who may feel disconnected from traditional political structures.

## Empowering Underserved Communities

Grassroots efforts frequently focus on empowering underrepresented groups, ensuring their voices are integrated into the electoral conversation. By offering resources, support, and education, these movements help individuals navigate the voting process and become actively engaged in civic life.

## Encouraging Voter Mobilization

Well-executed grassroots campaigns can significantly drive turnout by motivating supporters to vote and advocate for their preferred candidates. Effective messaging, community connections, and a sense of urgency surrounding critical issues can inspire individuals to participate in elections.

## Conclusion

Grassroots movements are vital in shaping the electoral landscape for the 2024 election, empowering communities and enhancing voter engagement. By leveraging social media, organizing impactful events, and concentrating on local concerns, these movements can generate support and drive meaningful change. As the election nears, the success of grassroots activism will be instrumental in influencing voter turnout and determining electoral outcomes.

# Chapter 8

## The Grassroots Movements' Lasting Influence on Democracy

As we wrap up the discussion on the 2024 election, it's essential to highlight the lasting influence of grassroots movements on the democratic process. These initiatives, rooted in local communities, have proven to be transformative forces, expanding voter participation and amplifying marginalized voices. Grassroots movements are not just fleeting strategies for elections; they embody the essence of democracy, fostering civic involvement and ensuring every voice counts.

## The Shift in Political Activism

Grassroots movements have evolved from traditional in-person organizing to incorporating digital platforms that connect with a wider audience. Social media has become a pivotal tool for activists, allowing movements to break geographic and demographic barriers, increasing their reach and impact.

- Digital vs. In-Person Engagement: While online organizing enables movements to grow rapidly, in-person interactions still play a critical role in building trust and personal connections within communities. These personal relationships often lead to long-term political engagement.

- Maintaining Momentum: After elections, keeping people involved remains a challenge. Movements that continue advocating for their causes after elections are vital in holding leaders accountable and ensuring progress continues.

## The Role of Grassroots in Future Elections

The success of grassroots campaigns in 2024 points to a larger trend in how elections will be conducted in the future. By prioritizing local issues and engaging voters directly, these movements redefine how political campaigns work, making politics more inclusive and transparent.

## Creating a Lasting Legacy of Civic Involvement

Grassroots efforts don't just focus on elections; they inspire ongoing civic participation. This sustained involvement encourages individuals to take an active role in policymaking, shaping a lasting legacy of engaged citizens who continue to influence their communities well beyond election day.

## Conclusion

Grassroots movements are a cornerstone of democracy, giving power to everyday citizens and promoting a healthier political system. The 2024 election has shown that these movements are capable of transforming the political landscape, ensuring that the government remains responsive to the people.

The true strength of grassroots activism lies in its ability to foster enduring participation, hold leaders accountable, and champion real change. Even after the ballots are counted, the lessons from grassroots movements will continue to shape the future of democracy, reminding us that democracy thrives when citizens remain informed, involved, and united by shared goals for the future.